Religious Education
in the Classroom

Book One

Christianity and Other World Faiths

by
E. Freedman and J. Keys

Published by
Prim-Ed Publishing

2850
REV–03/04

D1335866

Foreword

This series of books aims to provide teachers with a wide variety of activities which will support the Religious Education curriculum, whether Model 1 or Model 2 is being used. The materials will help develop knowledge and understanding of what it means to be a member of a faith community and how the teachings of these religions relate to shared human experience.

The activities were written to cover the attainment targets recommended for inclusion in an agreed syllabus.

Attainment Target 1: Learning about Religion

This includes the ability to:

- identify, name, describe and give accounts, in order to build a coherent picture of each religion;

- explain the meanings of religious language, stories and symbols; and

- explain similarities and differences between, and within, religions.

Attainment Target 2: Learning from Religion

This includes the ability to:

- give an informed and considered response to religious and moral issues;

- reflect on what might be learnt from religions in the light of one's own beliefs and experience; and

- identify and respond to questions of meaning within religions.

The materials aim to offer a coverage of the skills and processes in Religious Education, namely: investigation; interpretation; reflection; empathy; evaluation; analysis; synthesis; application; and expression. They can be used for whole class investigations and discussions, or by groups and pairs to engage in further research.

Fifty per cent of the activities within each book engage with Christianity; the remaining activities cover Buddhism, Hinduism, Islam, Judaism and Sikhism.

Contents

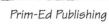

Teachers Notes

Christianity

1. Birthdays

Before doing the worksheet discuss how the children celebrate their own birthdays. Encourage them to see the reasons behind the parties and presents – a celebration of the life of someone who is much loved.

Draw a parallel with Christmas Day, the birthday of Jesus.

There is useful information in Celebrate Christian Festivals *by Jan Thompson, pub. Heinemann 1995.*

2. and 3. The Nativity

The stable picutre on Worksheet 3 and the figures on Worksheet 4 need to be stuck onto cardboard for strength. If children stick the background sheet onto the side of a complete cereal packet it will stand up easily and the nativity figures can be stored and taken home safely inside the box.

4. The Christmas Story

Read and discuss the Bible story of the birth of Jesus with the class then ask them to arrange the story in order. If you use long strips of paper they can be folded to make a concertina book.

Suitable books to read to the class include The Christmas Story *by Enid Blyton, republished by Red Fox 1993 or* The First Christmas *by Georgie Adams, pub. Orion 1996.*

5. My Christmas Alphabet

Encourage the children to think of a word or picture beginning with each letter of the alphabet that reminds them of the Christmas story. Younger children may need to be given words to copy before drawing their own picture.

For example: Advent, Bethlehem, Carol, Donkey, Eve, Frankincense, Gold, Holly, Ivy, Jesus, Kings, Lights, Mary, Nazareth, Oxen, Presents, the Queen (on TV!), Reindeer, Shepherds, Tree, Uncle, Visitors, Wenceslas, Xmas, Yule, Zzzzz.

6. Shrove Tuesday

Explain to the class about the kind of food that people would have eaten long ago, and why they chose to give up some foods for Lent. Permitted foods would have included bread, fish, beans and root vegetable (but no potatoes).

Discuss the children's favourite 'treat' foods and which of these a Christian might choose to give up for Lent.

Useful books include I am a Roman Catholic *by Brenda Pettenuzzo publ. Watts 1985 and* The Easter Story *by Brian Wildsmith pub. OUP 1993.*

7. Holy Week

Tell the class about the events of the last week of Jesus' life from the Gospels of Matthew, Ch.21 v. 1-13 and Ch.26 v. 17-29, and Luke Ch.21 v. 1-4.

Children can either cut out the pictures and text and glue them into their books in the correct sequence, or draw lines to link the pictures with the correct text.

Use a children's version such as The Easter Story *by David Hately pub. Ladybird 1990.*

8. Easter Words

Point out to the children that all the words in the crossword are symbols of new life in the Spring and the Easter message – daffodils, lambs, chicks, eggs and the Cross.

Read Easter *by Gail Gibbons pub. Hodder and Stoughton 1990.*

9. Easter Garden

Read a simple version of the Easter story to the class and point out the different locations mentioned.

If the local church has an Easter garden take the class to see it. Alternatively, the class could make an Easter garden either from plants and natural materials or using junk modelling techniques.

Read Brian Wildsmith's The Easter Story *pub. OUP 1993 or* The Easter Story *by David Hately publ. Ladybird 1990.*

Teachers Notes

10. Harvest Festival

Help the children identify the source of each of the foods shown. Discuss the tradition of thanking God for the harvest. Extend the work by asking children to consider where their favourite food comes from using the back of the worksheet.

You will find additional information in Celebrate Christian Festivals by Jan Thompson, pub. Heinemann 1995.

11. Mothering Sunday

Long before it was a commercial event there was a tradition of servant girls going home to visit their mothers on the middle Sunday in Lent with Gifts of Spring flowers or Simnel cakes. Include children who are not living with their mothers by encouraging them to make a card for the person that takes care of them. Fold the card twice so the flowers are on the front and the message inside.

12. The Bible

Show the class some examples of medieval illuminated manuscripts and discuss the amount of writing required to copy out the Bible. This can be linked with work on book-making and printing.

For a modern interpretation of illuminated manuscripts see The Chirstmas Story by Isabelle Brent pub. Pavillion 1989.

13. The Miracle of Jairus's Daughter

Tell the class the story of Jairus's daughter from Mark Ch.5 v. 22-43 and ask them to consider the feelings of the girl's parents.

14. The Good Samaritan

Re-tell the parable of the Good Samaritan from Luke Ch.10 v. 30-37, explaining that this is the story Jesus told to show people how they should treat each other.

15. The Good Shepherd

Re-tell the parable of the shepherd from Luke 15 v. 4-7. Show children pictures of sheep and shepherds, not necessarily from Biblical times, and discuss the work of shepherds.

Use Nick Butterworth and Mick Inkpen's delightful version The Lost Sheep pub. Marshall Pickering 1986.

16. Creation

Many cultures have legends about the creation of the world. You may like to compare this with other stories from South America, India and Australia.

The creation story is retold in Wonderful Earth! by Nick Butterworth and Mick Inkpen.

17. and 18. Outside a Church and a Wedding

Both worksheets are designed to make children familiar with the interior and exterior features of a traditional church building. The second also features a church ceremony. Ideally, these worksheets should be combined with a visit to a local church, or children could be shown pictures of churches.

Useful resources include The Usborne Book of World Religions by Susan Meredith pub. 1995, Discovering Churches by Lois Rock pub. Lion 1995 and Wedding by Lynne Hannigan pub. A & C Black 1988.

19. Christian Names

Children may need time at home to discuss why their names were chosen. Teachers must be sensitive to the feelings of children who do not have Christian names.

20. Sunday

This worksheet shows how Sunday is a special day for Christians. It can fit in with teaching the class about the days of the week.

21. Prayers

Ask the children if they know any prayers from school assembly or attending any religious services.

Discuss the kind of concerns that people might pray about.

Teachers Notes

22. Followers of Jesus

Give the children a brief outline of the lives of each of these Christians before asking them to identify them.

St Paul was from Tarsus, born a few years after Jesus and brought up in Jerusalem as a Jew. At first he persecuted the followers of Jesus but on the way to Damascus he had a vision of Jesus and converted to Christianity.

He was one of the founders of the early Church, travelling all round the eastern Mediterranean to preach about Jesus. The Epistles in the Bible are his letters to other Christians including the churches in Rome, Corinth and Ephesus.

See Saints *by Philip Sauvin pub. Wayland 1996.*

St Patrick was born in Wales towards the end of the fourth century. As a young man he was captured and taken to Ireland where he was a slave for about six years. He escaped to France and became a monk then went back to Ireland as a missionary.

He founded churches and monasteries and established the Church in Ireland.

See Patrick's Dream *by Cynthia and William Birrer pub. Julia MacRae 1989.*

St Francis was born in 1181, the son of a prosperous cloth merchant in Assisi, Italy. As a young man he had a vision that Jesus spoke to him from the cross in a ruined chapel and told him to repair the church.

He sold his horse, and his father's stock of cloth, wanting to give the money to the church. His father was angry and went to see the bishop. Francis took off all his rich clothing and gave them to his father saying that God was his father now. He gave up all his worldly goods and founded the Franciscan Order who dedicate themselves to a life of poverty. St. Francis loved nature and called all animals his brothers and sisters.

See St Francis: The Man who Spoke to Birds *by Georges Berton pub. Moonlight 1993.*

Mother Theresa was born in Albania in 1910 and lived in India where she founded the Missionaries of Charity. The nuns run hospitals and help very poor people who are homeless and dying in Calcutta, India. She died in 1997.

See Mother Theresa *by Charlotte Gray pub. Exley 1988.*

23. Stained Glass Window

The worksheet demonstrates some of the caring qualities that Jesus wanted Christians to follow.

Find some pictures of stained glass windows to show the class, or visit a local building with interesting windows.

Point out to the children the various Bible stories depicted in the stained glass window.

24. Have a Nice Day!

Discuss with the children ways in which they can make a contribution and show kindness to others. Children can draw or write in each sunshine circle and continue on the back of the sheet if necessary.

World Religions

25. Our Class

In discussing this work there are many opportunities for children to explore the faith communities represented amongst their classmates. Teachers will need to ensure this is done with respect and sensitivity. There is space to add an additional box if more categories are required.

This worksheet links in with National Curriculum mathematics on data handling. It could also be extended to cover other classes within the school.

Buddhism

26. Poya

Many children's books on Buddhism have colour photographs of Sri Lankan festivals including the Festival of the Tooth at Kandy in August, where a golden casket containing a relic of the Buddha is paraded through the streets. There are over a hundred decorated elephants similar to the ones below in this procession.

Useful books include Ananda in Sri Lanka *by Carol Barker pub. Hamish Hamilton,* I am a Buddhist *by Dhanapala and Udemi Samarasekara pub. Franklin Watts 1986 and* Buddhist Festivals *by John Snelling pub. Wayland 1985.*

Teachers Notes

27. The Five Vows

In considering these ancient Buddhist vows children many also like to think about drawing up rules for themselves in class.

28. Prayer

A popular mantra, or prayer, is *Om mani padme hum* which means 'the jewel in the lotus' or the truth at the heart of the teaching. Alternatively, children could compose their own prayer to write on the wheel.

As a technology task children could construct their own copies of the revolving bronze cylinders used in Tibetan Buddhist temples. Suitable materials might include cut halves of washing-up liquid bottles on sticks held vertical by modelling clay, or cardboard cylinders suspended on string.

See the Usborne Book of World Religions *by Susan Meredith pub. 1995.*

29. The Middle Way

This worksheet can be used within health educaiton to show the Buddhist message about the importance of moderation in all things for a healthy lifestyle.

Hinduism

30. Puja

Children could make a classroom replica of a domestic Hindu shrine like this, especially if it is possible to borrow items from local families.

See I am a Hindu *by Manju Aggarwal pub. Watts 1984.*

31. Ganesh and Hanuman

There are many stories about these two popular gods that children would enjoy hearing.

In the Ramayana it was Hanuman the monkey god who helped Rama to rescue Sita from Ravana. He did many marvellous deeds including setting fire to a city with his tail, and carrying a whole mountain from the Himalayas. His monkeys held hands to make a bridge from India to Sri Lanka.

Diwali *by Beulah Candappa pub. Ginn 1985 gives a simple version of the story.*

32. Divali

The Divali festival in the Autumn offers many opportunities for art work including drawing and colouring Rangoli patterns and making diva lamps from clay or modelling clay.

Hindu communities have different traditions for Divali. Some link it with Rama and Sita's return, others with Lakshmi, but it is always a happy festival with plenty of bright lights and fireworks.

See Diwali *by Chris Deshpande pub. A & C Black 1985.*

33. The Story of the Elephant

This is a traditional story told to explain the many facets of Hindu belief across the subcontinent. Each of the blind men is right about the part of the elephant that he can feel, none of them have got the overall picture. The children could act out this story as a drama, and try to think of other ways of describing the elephant.

The story is retold in The Usborne Book of World Religions *by Susan Meredith pub. 1995.*

Islam

34. Eid al Fitr

This is one of the major Muslim festivals, much enjoyed by the children. It is marked by the first appearance of the new moon at the end of the lunar month of Ramadan.

See I am a Muslim *by Clive Lawton pub. Watts 1980-84.*

35. Muhammad

Muslims tell this story about how the spider wove a web across the cave mouth and the dove sat on her nest to help Muhammad hide from his enemies.

Remind the children how long it takes for a spider to make a web, and that birds will not usually nest near people.

Muslims would be very offended by any attempt to draw Muhammad himself.

Teachers Notes

36. Patterns

When the children have coloured these Islamic designs they may be able to draw patterns of their own, especially if they are able to refer to illustrations in books.

Children can compare the Islamic style of religious art with the Christian tradition of pictures of Jesus, Mary and the saints.

For illustrations see Inside Story – A 16th Century Mosque *by Fiona Macdonald pub. Simon and Schuster 1994.*

37. Prayer

It is one of the fundamental duties of Muslims to pray five times a day. No matter where they happen to be, they should wash, take off their shoes, spread out a small prayer mat and pray in the direction of Mecca.

Judaism

38. Hanuka

Hanuka is a happy festival for Jewish families, which falls just before Christmas.

It commemorates the victory of Judas Maccabeus and his guerilla fighters over the Greek army of Antiochus in around 150 BC.

The Temple in Jerusalem had been defiled by the worship of idols and slaughter of pigs. It was important for the Jews to relight the Temple lamps but they found there was only a little oil, enough for one day. The miracle of Hanuka is that God kept the lamp burning for eight days until more oil could be fetched.

Hanuka candles like this are lit at dusk each evening, using the shammash or servant candle to light the others, one more each night, starting at the right hand end of the line.

Some Jewish communities have traditional foods at this time, often fried in oil. There are traditional glames using a special wooden top called a dreidel, and children may receive presents or money (Hanuka gelt).

Useful books include Hanukka *by Leila Berg pub. Ginn 1985 and* Hanukkah Fun *by Judy Bastyra and Catherine Ward pub. Kingfisher 1996.*

39. and 40. Joseph

This is a story from the Old Testament which is sacred to both Jews and Christians. It is told in CH. 37-50 of the Book of Genesis but there are many more appropriate versions for children. The story may already be familiar from the musical Joseph and the Amazing Technicolour Dreamcoat.

Refer Joseph the Long Lost Brother *retold by Catherine Storr pub. Franklin Watts 1985.*

41. Sabbath

When discussing other special holy days with the class, notice that Jews take their seventh day of rest on Saturday not Sunday. Also, the Sabbath begins when it gets dark on Friday and ends at dusk on Saturday.

See I am a Jew *by Clive Lawton pub. Watts London/Sydney 1985.*

Sikhism

42. Sharing

This worksheet is intended as an introduction to the vocabulary of the Sikh community. If possible children should have an opportunity to discuss this with a Sikh.

The concept of sharing food together as equals is very important to the Sikh way of life, and should be stressed in class discussions.

43. The Five Ks

When Guru Gobind Singh founded the Khalsa, or brotherhood of Sikhs, he said all members should wear these five symbols of their faith. Long uncut hair (kesh) is often a sign of holiness in India, but Sikhs must keep theirs clean and comb it regularly using a kanga. Men usually cover their hair with a turban. The kara is a bangle made of steel, the circle is a symbol of unity and that God has no beginning or end. The kirpan is a sword to remind Sikhs that they are warriors fighting to defend their beliefs; nowadays a very small symbolic sword is worn. Finally, the kachha are simple cotton shorts that Sikhs were told to wear instead of the normal long skirt-like dhoti because it was easier to move and fight in shorts. Modern Sikhs wear these as underwear.

See I am a Sikh *by Manju Aggarwal pub. Franklin Watts.*

Teachers Notes

44. The Guru's Special Cloak

This is a very popular story about the sixth Guru, or leader, of the Sikhs who lived from 1595 to 1644, during the reign of the Emperor Jehangir, and was imprisoned at Gwalior Fortress. When the Guru was released with all the Hindu princes he returned to Amritsar where the Sikhs greeted him with candles. Sikhs remember this story at the Hindu festival of Divali and send Divali cards.

You will find this and other stories in Stories from the Sikh World *by Rami and Jugnu Singh pub. Macdonald 1987.*

44. Names

The names used in Sikh families have great religious significance. A new baby is taken to a service a the gurdwara as soon as possible and after music and prayers the Guru Granth Sahib is opened at random. The first letter of the shabad (poem) on the left-hand page becomes the first letter of the child's name. The parents then choose a name and the Granthi announces it to the congregation, adding Singh for a boy or Kaur for a girl.

Discuss with the children why they think Sikh parents might want their daughters to be like princesses and their sons like lions.

World Religions

46. Beads

Some children may already be familiar with prayer beads and could bring some in to show the class. Alternatively, children could make their own using wooden or papier mâché beads.

47. and 48. Signs of Faith

Ideally, children should have an opportunity to visit local places of worship and look for the religious symbols displayed there. Where this is not possible they can be shown how to find the information in illustrated reference books.

Christians worship in a church and their symbol is the cross upons which Jesus was crucified.

 **Buddhists** worship in a temple and their symbol is the wheel of life, symbolising their belief in reincarnation.

Hindu places of worship are also called temples. Their sacred symbol is the Hindu word Om.

Jews worship in a synagogue and their symbol is the Star of David, a great King in the Bible.

Muslims worship in a mosque and their symbol is the crescent moon, they use a lunar calendar.

 **Sikhs** worship in a gurdwara and their symbol shows two crossed swords and a bangle, two of the five Ks that all Sikhs carry.

note:

When dealing with religions other than Christianity it is customary not to use BC and AD for dates. BCE (Before the Common Era) is used for BC and CE (Common Era) for AD.

Birthdays

☆ *Fill in the blank spaces.*

My birthday is on _____ .

I was born _____ years ago.

My family and friends celebrate my birthday by...

_____

_____

_____

_____

Christmas is on

_____ .

Jesus was born _____ years ago.

Christians celebrate the birthday of Jesus by...

_____

_____

_____

_____

My Christmas Alphabet

Put a word or picture in each box that makes you think of Christmas.

Aa	Bb	Cc	Dd	Ee
Ff	Gg	Hh	Ii	Jj
Kk	Ll	Mm	Nn	Oo
Pp	Qq	Rr	Ss	Tt
Uu	Vv	Ww	Xx	Yy
Zz				

Holy Week

☆ *Join each picture to the correct sentence then colour the pictures.*

Jesus explained that the Widow's tiny coins were worth more to God than the money the rich men gave because she gave all she had.

•   •

Jesus drove out the money-changers and traders who were turning the Temple from a place for quiet prayer into a den of thieves.

•   •

Jesus and his disciples ate their last meal together and Jesus told them how to remember him with bread and wine when he had gone.

•   •

On Palm Sunday Jesus rode into Jerusalem on a donkey and the crowds cheered and waved palm branches to greet him.

•   •

Harvest Festival

At Harvest Festival we say thank you to God for the food we eat.

☆ Join the pictures to show where our food comes from.

☆ Draw and write about your favourite meal.

My favourite food is _____

_____

Christians have a holy book called the Bible with lots of different stories in it. Four followers of Jesus wrote about his life. These stories are called the Gospels.

Before the invention of printing monks used to copy the Bible and decorate the pages by hand, as shown on this page.

Colour in the cards of Gospel decorations.

Do you know any stories from the Gospels?

The Miracle of Jairus's Daughter

Listen to the story of Jairus and his daughter.

☆ *What did her father say when she woke up?*

_____

_____

_____

☆ *What did her mother say when she woke up?*

_____

_____

_____

☆ *What did Jesus say?*

_____

_____

_____

The Good Samaritan

Jesus told this story.

☆ *Read it, and colour the pictures.*

On the way to Jericho a man was attacked by robbers who beat him up and took all he had.

A priest came by. When he saw the wounded man he crossed the road and hurried past.

Next, an important man from the city came by. He looked at the wounded man then walked on.

But the Samaritan felt sorry for the man so he stopped and gave him first aid.

Then he put the wounded man on his own donkey and took him somewhere he could rest.

The Samaritan left some money to pay for the man to be cared for until he was well again.

Which person do you think Jesus wants us to copy?

_____

Why? _____

_____

The Good Shepherd

Jesus says that God is like a good shepherd who will always look after his sheep.

When at last he found the lost sheep, he was very happy. He carried her home and told all his friends.

It was cold and dark, but he left the other sheep safe for the night and went off to look for the one that was lost.

Once upon a time there was a shepherd who had a hundred sheep. One night he counted and there were only ninety-nine.

Read the story. Draw your own pictures.

The Bible says that God created Heaven and Earth in six days.

☆ *Draw the things God made each day.*

On the first day God made light so there was night and day.

On the second day God made the sea and the sky.

On the third day God made the dry land and the plants and trees.

On the fourth day God made the sun and the moon.

On the fifth day God made the fish in the sea and the birds in the air.

On the sixth day God made the animals and then made Adam and Eve, the first people.

And on the seventh day, God rested.
So Christians say Sunday is a day of rest.

02/08

Easter Words

Easter is a Spring festival when we think about new life.

☆ Fill in the Easter words in this crossword.

E
A
S
T
E
R

Outside a Church

☆ Fill in all the labels on the church then colour the picture.

steeple

tombstone

cross

graveyard

stained glass window

bell tower

A **W**edding

Have you ever been to a wedding?

When a man and a woman get married in church they promise to love and look after each other all their lives.

☆ Draw a line from the name to the correct part of the wedding ceremony in the church. Colour the picture.

bride   bridesmaid   groom   vicar

pulpit   altar   pews   organ

Sundays

Christians keep Sunday as their special holy day.

Children may go to Sunday School to learn about their religion.

Adults go to a church service in the morning or evening.

☆ *Fill in the days of the week and colour the pictures.*

M

T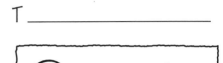

W _____

T _____

F _____

S _____

S _____

Prayers

A prayer is a way of talking to God. There are different ways of praying. Sometimes Christians say a prayer together, like this one before a meal:

For what we are about to receive

May the Lord make us truly thankful.

Amen.

Or the vicar says the prayer and the people say AMEN.

Sometimes Christians pray just by sitting quietly and thinking. Here are some ideas for prayers. Think of some other things you might want to sit and think about quietly.

☆ Draw a picture for each idea.

My family

People who are hungry

My friends

There are many famous Christians who try to follow the example of Jesus.

☆ Read about these four people then write their names and colour the pictures.

This is a picture of

_____

This is a picture of

_____

This is a picture of

_____

This is a picture of

_____

St Francis was a rich young Italian who became a poor monk. He loved animals and birds.

Mother Theresa looked after poor people in Calcutta, India.

St Paul wrote letters to the first churches telling them how to live a Christian life.

St Patrick went to Ireland to tell the people about Jesus.

A Stained Glass Window

Christians learn about the life of Jesus and try to follow his example.

1. Jesus shared with others.

2. Jesus cared for the sick.

3. Jesus was a friend to children.

4. Jesus prayed to God.

☆ *Write on each different stained-glass window the things Jesus did. Colour each window.*

☆ *Think about how we can do these things.*

Have a Nice Day!

How could you brighten up the day for those around you?

☆ write inside each sun all the things you could do.

Family

Teacher

Friends

Pets

Our Class

In Mrs Smith's class the children have many different religions.

Mallika is a Buddhist

Sara is a Muslim.

Sam is a Jew.

Rajiv is a Hindu.

Kate is a Christian.

Harmandip is a Sikh.

☆ Ask the children in your class about their religion. Put a X in the correct box for each child.

Buddhist	
Christian	
Hindu	
Jew	
Muslim	
Sikh	

Poya

Dress the other elephants for the festival. Draw the moon.

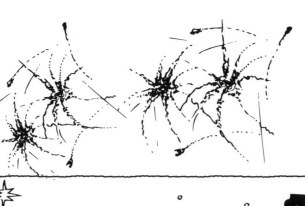

In Sri Lanka the Buddhists celebrate full moon days with big parades.

The Five Vows

Mallika's family repeat these promises in front of a statue of Buddha at home every day.

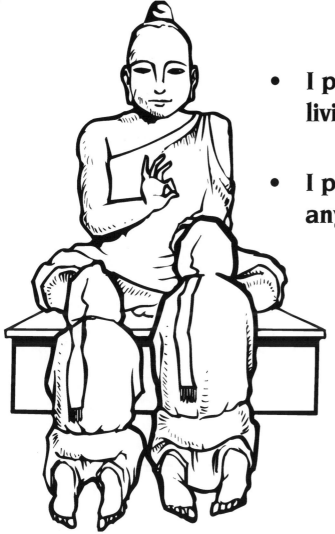

- **I promise not to harm any living thing.**

- **I promise not to take anything not given to me.**

- **I promise to keep calm.**

- **I promise not to say anything unkind.**

- **I promise to keep a clear head.**

Buddhists have made these promises for thousands of years. Can they help us today?

Write five promises for yourself.

1. I promise _____

2. I promise _____

3. I promise _____

4. I promise _____

5. I promise _____

In Tibet the Buddhists write prayers on cylinders. Each spin of the wheel is a prayer.

Sometimes they write on a banner so the wind will blow their prayers.

Write your own prayer on this banner.

The Middle Way

This is how Buddha found the Middle Way.

Once there was a prince called Siddhartha who lived in great comfort in a palace, doing no work and eating and drinking as much as he wanted.

Then Siddhartha left his palace and went off to be a holy man, wearing rags, sleeping by the roadside and eating only a grain of rice a day.

But then he saw there was a Middle Way. He became a famous teacher - the Buddha.

1. What happens if you eat too much? _____

_____

2. Or if you eat too little? _____

_____

3. What happens if you do too little work? _____

_____

4. Or if you do too much? _____

_____

Buddha says we must find the Middle Way.

In Rajiv and Sita's home there is a shrine like this for puja - worship. There is something there to please all the senses.

Join each part of the shrine to the part of the body you will use to enjoy it. Colour the shrine.

Ganesh and Hanuman

Hindus have many gods.

This is Hanuman who helped Prince Rama to rescue his lovely wife Sita.

Ganesh is the son of Shiva and his wife Parvati. When he lost his head, his father gave him a different one.

Colour in the pictures of Ganesh and Hanuman and fill in the questions below.

Look out for Ganesh with the head of an _____ .

Look out for Hanuman with the head of a _____ .

🕉 *Draw a line between the sentence in the box and its matching picture.*

Rangoli patterns make the house look special for Divali.

Sita enjoys the Divali fireworks.

At the Divali festival Hindus welcome the goddess Lakshmi.

The special Divali oil lamps are called Diva.

The Story of the Elephant

Hinduism began in India many years ago. Hindus have different stories about the gods and worship them in different ways. This story explains how people can all have their own ideas and yet all be right.

 Fill in the speech balloons to show what each of the blind men think an elephant is like.

a rope

a wall

a snake

a spear

a fan

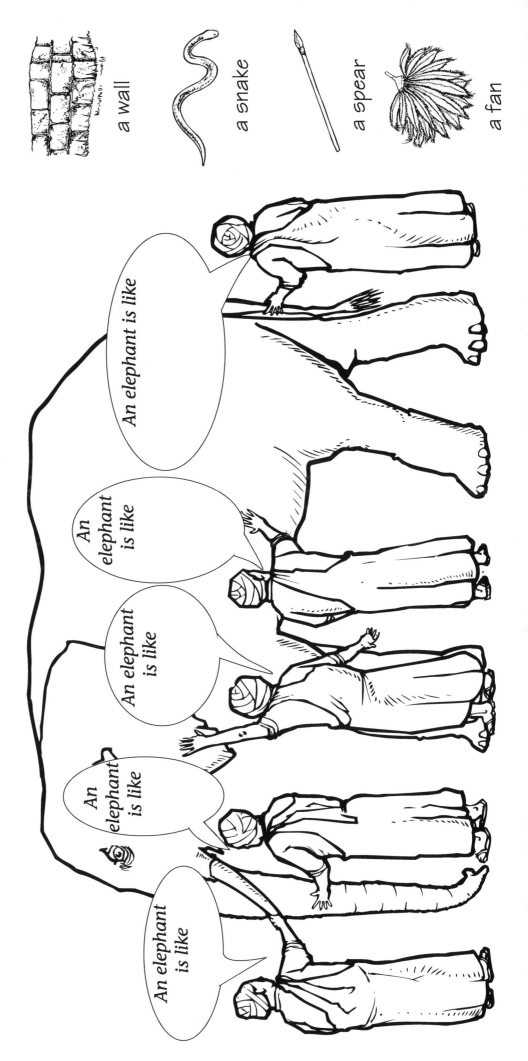

Eid al Fitr

During the month of Ramadan adults in Sara and Rahman's family do not eat all day.

The new moon tells them Ramadan is over and they can celebrate the festival of Eid al Fitr.

Sara and Rahman get new clothes and toys. There will be a special meal and lots of sweets.

Draw the night sky with the new moon at Eid al Fitr.

Draw the food Rahman and Sara will eat for their Eid al Fitr feast.

Draw a toy for Rahman at Eid al Fitr.

Draw some new clothes for Sara to wear at Eid al Fitr.

Muhammad

☪ *Read the story of how Muhammad escaped from Mecca to Medina then complete the picture.*

Once, when Muhammad and Abu Bakr were escaping from Mecca they hid in a cave.

Soldiers came to look for them, but when they saw a spider web across the cave mouth and a dove on her nest they went away.

☪ *Draw the bird in her nest and the spider web across the cave mouth. Remember Muslims never make pictures of Muhammad.*

Why did the soldiers think Muhammad and his friends were not in the cave?

Because _____

_____

Muslims do not make pictures of their god Allah or of his prophet Muhammad.

They make beautiful patterns like this to decorate their holy buildings which are called mosques.

Sometimes they make patterns with their writing. This is the word Muhammed in Arabic.

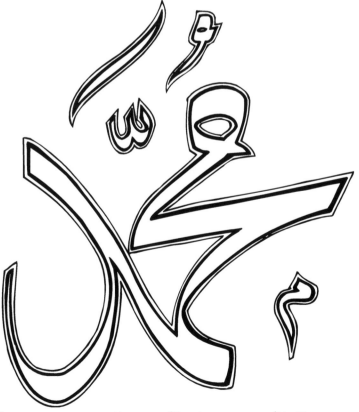

Colour in the patterns. Try making your own patterns with shapes or with the letters in your name.

Prayer

What have you learned about Muslim prayers? Circle the correct answers.

Questions about Muslim Prayers

How often do Muslims pray?	Once a week Every day Five times a day
Which way do Muslims face?	Towards home Towards Mecca North
When do Muslims wash?	After prayers Before prayers At bedtime
Where do Muslims pray?	Only at the mosque In the living room Anywhere
What do Muslims take off to pray?	Hats Coats Shoes

Colour the pattern on the prayer mat.

Hanuka

At the Hanuka festival Jews remember how they won back the Temple in Jerusalem from their enemies. There was very little oil - enough for one night - but God kept the Temple light burning for eight days.

Jewish families light special Hanuka candles each evening.

✡ *Draw the candles and complete the sentences.*

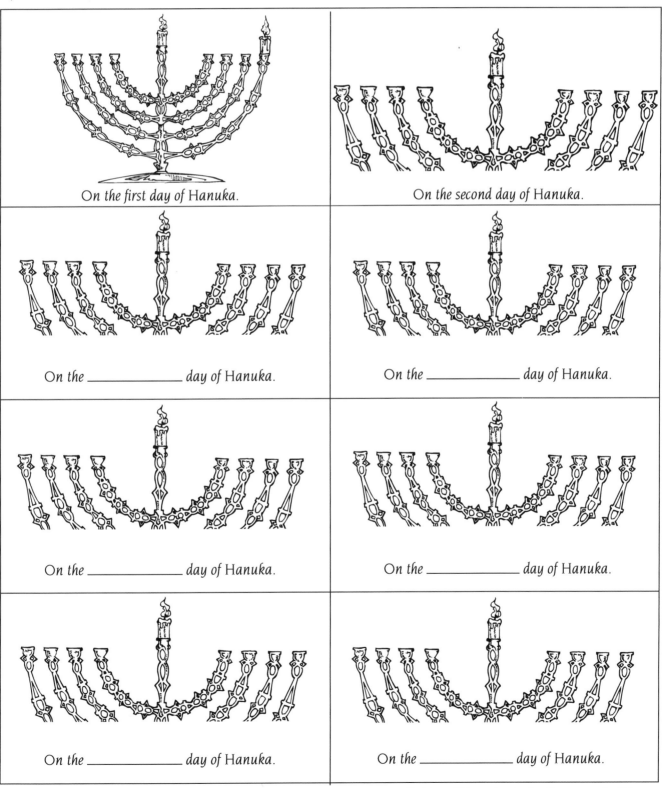

On the first day of Hanuka.

On the second day of Hanuka.

On the _____ day of Hanuka.

On the _____ day of Hanuka.

On the _____ day of Hanuka.

On the _____ day of Hanuka.

On the _____ day of Hanuka.

On the _____ day of Hanuka.

The Bible says that Jacob had twelve sons but he loved Joseph best. He made a special colourful coat for Joseph.

Joseph told his brothers that in his dream they all bowed down to him.

✡ *How do you think the brothers felt?*
Fill in the speech bubbles and colour in Joseph's coat.

I had a strange dream...

Joseph's brothers sent him off to Egypt as a slave.

Joseph — Part Two

✡ Cut the text boxes out below and glue in the right order in the squares.
Draw pictures to match each piece of text and make a book.

Back at home, Jacob and his other sons were hungry. They came to Egypt to beg for food. They didn't recognise Joseph.	Joseph told the King of Egypt that his dreams meant they must store food for the years ahead when harvests would be bad.
Joseph invited his whole family to come and live with him in Egypt.	Joseph was a slave in Egypt. Then his master sent him to prison. He could foretell the future from dreams.

Find out about Sam's family's special holy day each week.

✡ *Fill in the missing words using the list below.*

The _____ starts at _____ on

_____ when my mum lights the

_____ . We say Shabbat

Shalom — have a

_____

Sabbath.

No-one in the family does any _____ on the Sabbath. We go

to _____ then relax until it gets

_____ on _____ .

(**Sabbath**)   (**sunset**)   (**Friday**)   (**candles**)   (**peaceful**)

(**work**)   (**synagogue**)   (**dark**)   (**Saturday**)

✡ *Do you have a special day of rest in your family?*

Sharing

Fill in the missing words using the list below.

Harmandip and his family are _____. They go to the

_____ to listen to music and hear readings

from the _____ _____ _____ , their

holy book.

Guru Granth Sahib

langar

share

Gurdwara

children

Sikhs

eats

Afterwards everyone _____ together in the

_____ . Even _____

can help prepare the meal. Sikhs believe it is very

important to _____ .

Who shares food with you? _____

Sikhs have five special ways to show that they are following their Gurus.

All the words begin with the '**k**' sound in Punjabi.

🪯 *Write the Punjabi word below under each picture.*

k

Kesh - long, uncut hair		**Kanga** - comb
Kirpan - sword		**Kara** - steel bracelet
Kachha - cotton shorts		

The Guru's Special Cloak

Match the pictures with the sentences.

1. Guru Har Govind was once put in prison. When Emperor Jehanjir heard this, he said 'Set the Guru free.'

2. But there were fifty-two rajahs in Gwalior fort with the Guru. He did not want to leave them behind in prison.

3. The Emperor said that the Guru could free anyone who was holding on to his cloak when he went through the prison gate.

4. So Guru Har Govind wore a special long cloak with fifty-two tassels, and all the rajahs walked out of the prison with him.

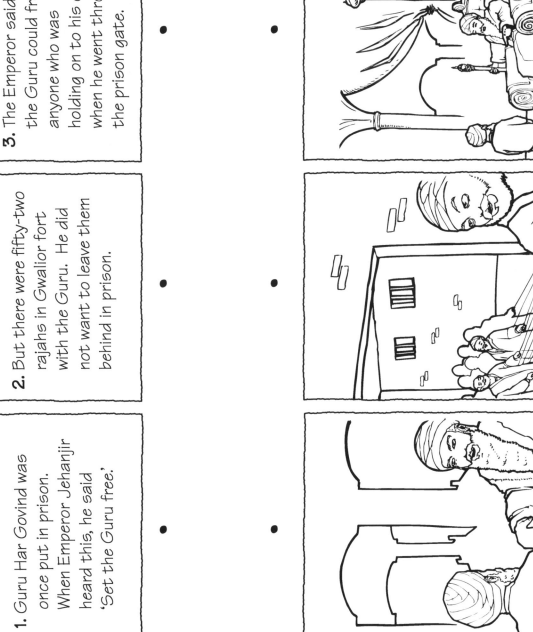

Sikh parents find a name for their new baby by opening their holy book — the Guru Granth Sahib — and looking for the first letter at the top of the left-hand page. They then choose a name that begins with that letter.

Try this yourself with a book and write below.

Girls Names

_____

_____

_____

_____

_____

Boys Names

_____

_____

_____

_____

_____

All Sikh girls have Kaur in their name. It means Princess.

All Sikh boys have Singh in their name. It means Lion.

Beads

Many different religions use prayer beads.

☆ You can make your own beads. Each one means something special for you. Write what is special to you on the beads below and colour them.

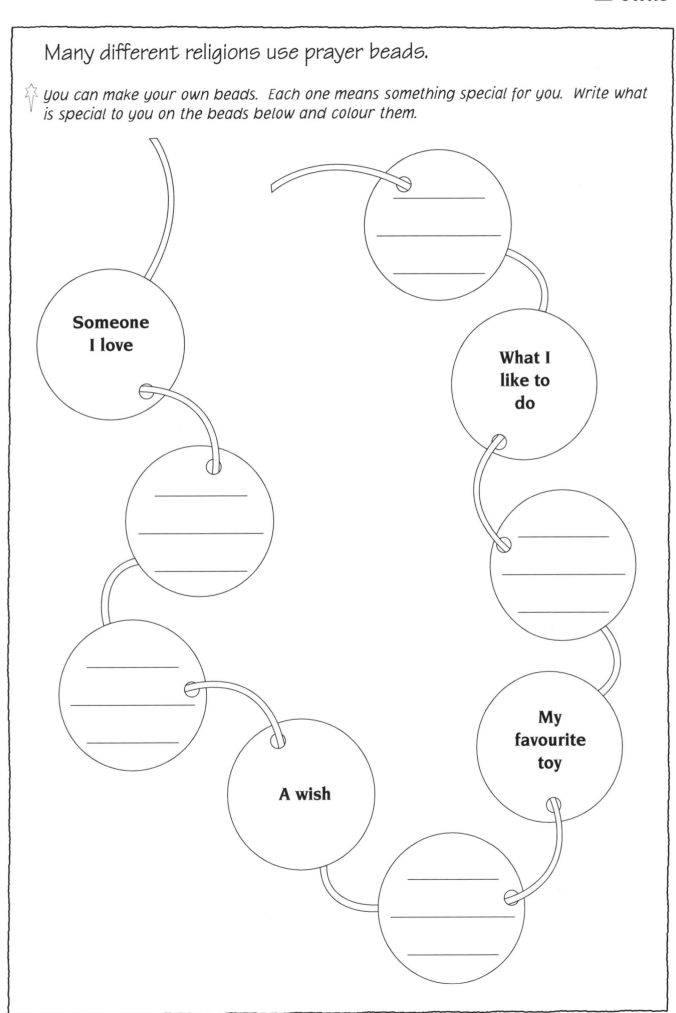

Someone I love

What I like to do

My favourite toy

A wish

Signs of Faith — Part one

Mosque

Buddhist temple

Hindu temple

Church

Synagogue

Gurdwara

Signs of Faith — *Part two*

Christians go to	**Their symbol is**
Buddhists go to	**Their symbol is**
Hindus go to	**Their symbol is**
Jews go to	**Their symbol is**
Muslims go to	**Their symbol is**
Sikhs go to	**Their symbol is**

Answers

Page 6   Shrove Tuesday
Lent, Tuesday, pancakes, fast

Page 7   Holy Week
*Pictures, top to bottom, match with
text:*
- *On Palm Sunday ...*
- *Jesus and his disciples ...*
- *Jesus drove out ...*
- *Jesus explained ...*

Page 8   Easter Words
egg, lamb, chicks, rabbit, flower, cross

Page 10   Harvest Festival
*milk – cow, bread – wheat, apple –
tree, strawberry – plant*

Page 17   Outside a Church

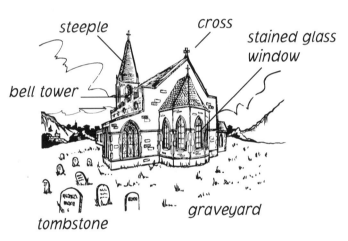

Page 18   A Wedding

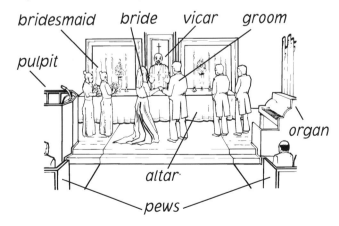

Page 22   Followers of Jesus
*Top to bottom: St Francis, Mother
Theresa, St Patrick, St Paul*

Page 31   Ganesh and Hanuman
Ganesh – elephant, Hanuman – monkey

Page 33   The Story of the Elephant
*Left–right: a spear; a snake; a fan; a
wall; a rope*

Page 37   Prayer
*five times a day, towards Mecca,
before prayers, anywhere, shoes*

Page 41   Sabbath
*Sabbath, sunset, Friday, candles,
peaceful, work, synagogue, dark,
Saturday*

Page 42   Sharing
*Sikhs, Gurdwara, Guru Granth Sahib,
eats, langar, children, share*

Page 48   Signs of Faith
Christians, Church, Cross

Buddhists, Temple, Wheel of Life

Hindus, Temple, Hindu word 'Om'

Jews, Synagogue, Star of David

Muslims, Mosque, Crescent Moon

*Sikhs, Gurdwara, Two crossed swords
and a bangle*